While Crossing the Field

DEBORAH BANKS

for Barbara and Max

With gratitude for all the
goodness and warmth you bring
to our rural community. How
brightly you shine in the world!

Warmly,

Deborah

POTTERSFIELD PRESS
Lawrencetown Beach, Nova Scotia, Canada

Library and Archives Canada Cataloguing in Publication

Title: While crossing the field / Deborah Banks.

Names: Banks, Deborah, 1961- author.

Description: Poems.

Identifiers: Canadiana (print) 20200172808 | Canadiana (ebook) 20200201239 | ISBN 9781989725139

   (softcover) | ISBN 9781989725146 (PDF)

Classification: LCC PS8603.A6235 W55 2020 | DDC C811/.6—dc23

Cover image: 123rf stock image (fotolesnik)

Cover design by Gail LeBlanc

Pottersfield Press gratefully acknowledges the financial support of the Government of Canada for our publishing activities. We also acknowledge the support of the Canada Council for the Arts and the Province of Nova Scotia which has assisted us to develop and promote our creative industries for the benefit of all Nova Scotians.

Pottersfield Press
248 Leslie Road
East Lawrencetown, Nova Scotia, Canada, B2Z 1T4
Website: www.PottersfieldPress.com
To order, phone 1-800-NIMBUS9 (1-800-646-2879) www.nimbus.ns.ca

Printed in Canada

Pottersfield Press is committed to preserving the environment and the appropriate harvesting of trees and has printed this book on Forest Stewardship Council® certified paper.

for my gentle-hearted parents

*"Poets have found religion in nature;
people live in the country to learn virtue
from plants."*

– Virginia Woolf

Contents

Spring Fever

1.

Flickers forage in the spring rain, beaks down,
male and female, punching earth's teeming time clock.
They drift up the hill, and then are gone.
All morning the heavy rains. Time drags on
in a good way, a day that never ends.
Dirt roads soften and tug at tires.
The clay soil loosens in my fingers.
My rubber boots are thick with fresh mud –
the cloying earth swallows their choked treads.
My face stained with the grainy beauty of it.
The wind blows winter's last proposal away.

2.

Cutting across the field to my sister's
tonight I notice the greening of our trail
and, in the distance, the height of the tide.
The spring dampness is in the air.
A quiet car passes, perhaps one an hour.
Old man's beard lifts in the fog
from distended branches of weary coastal spruce.
Smoke rises from chimneys, just a smudge
to take out the chill, winter's last taunt.
The land is coming together now.
I release myself into these days,
interrupt thoughts that do not prosper,
and bend my quickening ear to the land.

3.

So much noise! At once the cacophonous
chorus of wooing birds from the yard
and on the telephone wire they vie
for nooks in the hollows of the poles.
Even the dear robin whose mighty heart
is thrumming a thousand beats a minute
pitches his love corridor into the air,
measuring the room and announcing walls.
We, too, once loved like this, our young bodies
knowing no boundaries.

4.

When I stood outside tonight at dusk,
the moon ghosted between scudding clouds
and the peepers, those gangsters of noise,
threw their voices across the lake.
A crow with a stick pinched in his beak
overshot the trees by the stone wall
and carried on to the ocean shore.
Everything in its place, everything moving,
animate and doing, its great doing
despite everything, despite us.
This bliss is easy, untroubled by the world.
We go on thinking we'll go on.

Freeing the Stone Wall

The long bales of rusty wire
brittle with time's slogging increments
crumble in my hands. They come away
grudgingly, ensnared in small trees and bramble.
The steadfast moss against tree trunks bears witness
as fractured bottles wedged beneath stones detach
the exhalation of corroded lives
where lichen remains a benign bracelet along the wall.

When the wire is gone, the rich musky earth
is exposed, and I pat it with my hands
its renewed life on fire in my fists.
The relief – is it mine? Not entirely.
We collude in a shared restfulness
that is wide and untranslatable.

Sap Moon of March

This morning: a trinity of workhorses forms a pastiche
on a marbled landscape in Brome.
They stand facing into the sun –
the glorious returning light of March!
In this new wideness, farmhouse eaves drip
to softening patches of earth,
the seeds reawaken,
their bright eyes blinking open at last.

All this devotion to rekindled warmth,
the renewal of spring on skin, coat, bark.
In the woods beyond, the sap
is coursing through the veins of the maples,
chugging invisible tap lines
under the ground, each waking up the other.

But by afternoon, in my childhood village,
the mighty pine trees my mother and I loved
for half a century have been cut down.
Those centenarians have been toppled.
They are blunt remains on a ruined landscape.
The thick moss trails where we paused on our walks,
the homage we paid to those mighty warriors,
is a memory gone horribly rancid.

And now the sap moon of late March
is weighted with new meaning.
Such unscrupulous husbandry.

My heart is soured by human endeavour
in a lonely world that forgets
what devotion could mean.

Into the Darkening Night

Into the darkening night
from the kitchen window
I see the patches of more shadow
where the snow has melted
and left scrapings of earth
and where I uncovered the ground
for the birds
and they scrambled earlier
to scratch at the grass
and find old seed and new life.

We will forever be looking
into the darkness, won't we?
The rapture of triumph, our noble moments
and those miscarriages of decisions
with their murky stains
merging together,
where one begins and the other ends
forever cancelling the other out.

The land will not catalogue this human acreage.

Conversation with a Weasel

This morning in the woodpile
the tiny tufted head of an immature weasel
pops up to study my movements.

Who is more curious about the world, I wonder?

Today the sun is unfolding spring's story
and we are both feverish with the thrill of it!
The hard tracks in the road are giving way to mud,
the song of the birds is filling the trees again,
and I am gathering wood for the last clutches of heat
in these days of longer light.

How uncomplicated is that life?

Too often my world is measured in strife and cares.
Meanwhile the weasel scavenges the new bird nests,
all those vulnerable cottages in the branches.
It is a heartbreak and a truth that settles in me,
but the love of truth is going to win.

The curious weasel studying me
between the slats of wood pallets
reminds me
that there is only the infinity
of this great moment,
the dwelling place
where we recognize each other's strangeness.

Loons in April

At last the loons have returned to the land.
Quietly coupled, they drift on a soft wake.
I have missed their hollowed winnowing
and the weighted aftereffects of it,
how my life in those moments is enlarged
and diminished simultaneously.

The riddling universe is asking us
to consider this sharp duality.
Both moments are the other and neither;
the loss in the loon's call and what is found
in the residue of the silence after,
the deep wrinkles growing in my skin
and the fact that it does not matter –
only the lake echoes now and always.

Catalogue

The long thunder of the ocean
is rolling along the shore.
I can think, in some moments,
it is all I ever wanted.

But then I remember the musky smell
of the woods today,
the trail mossy and tempted by spring,
and I might think: This is enough.

Both equals.

And then the stars tonight
breaking their familiar canvas
with light.

Well, it could be that.

On the Back Hill

On the back hill
all early morning
the doe ate fresh tufts of green
raising her head
to watch me watch her
the whiskers on her chin
dew-wet and lit by the sun
so that I laugh out loud
as she chews sideways
and stares back.
Even with my admonishment
to be mistrustful of humans
she does not stir.

Then later, both mourning doves
arrive as my sister said they would –
two halves of a whole.

If I did not have these moments
I would forget that I love my life.

Lost Bird

for Laura

"Are you still thinking about that bird?"
my sister asks.

We both are. What we could have done.

After the storm, we pulled into the beach parking
to watch the surge gnaw at the shore,
swamp the grasses
and overpower the brook, now swollen and bloated.

And there he was: a foreign bird, blown off-course,
paddling against the exertions of the sea.
Disoriented, that brown-tufted head
drifted, swam, drifted, swam.
He stumbled to the ice on the bank
then dropped himself back in the brook
and disappeared up the stream
to the lake head where a wide gash of water
had opened with the thrust of the ocean,
everything backing up.

We did nothing.

We drove away in grey skies,
the windows still rolled down
and the roar following us up the winding road
like a dragon's exhaled breath, a yawning monster
that giant sea,
the lost and tossed birds with their crooked wings
unfolding behind us.

Night Sky, Again

When I come home and look up
the stars have punctured the night sky;
those points of light
illuminate the darkness
from horizon to horizon.
The Milky Way,
that measureless pioneer of mystery
with its long tracts of chalk,
multiplies as we breathe.

And the knowing peepers,
from the warming murk of ponds below,
are casting their music into smooth night air,
charting earthly patterns
to echo the vaulted dome.

The hungry molecules in me
thrill with recognition.
The greatness of it.

My heart quickens to bursting
that I can love this well.

Spring Along the Stone Wall

The wakening earth is growing outward:
spring delivers the new birthing of stones
out of the loins of trees and in the ditch,
and crammed inside an old moss-covered tire:
four unbroken beer and hooch bottles,
lost histories shepherded into the world
exposed and dampened by an impartial ground.
Bob's old wire fences now buttress air
and the crockery that failed the kitchen
is wedged beneath sage-green lichen, staring up.
Finally, along the stone wall
in a pool of water by a windfall tree
I find an egg, intact, cold and condemned:
an ancestral voice that will never speak.

Coming Home

for Bonnie

The geese are coming home.
I say it with relief as I make
my way to the train station and notice
their familiar formations
mustering along the horizon.

For days we have been buried in snow
where even the lengthening light
was dimmed in the tempest
that surrounded my parents' house.

My sister, ill with radiation treatments,
has spent most of her days in bed.
I have sat with her
sometimes touching her skin,
exploring the unexpected sharpness of her temple
where surgery changed her face forever.
When at last I climb the stairs to say goodbye,
she holds my hand and strokes it over and over.
We settle into a place
where circumstance
has made room for tenderness.

Now, from the train this morning,
a world that spring has overlooked:
I stare out at the Matapedia River
buried under a landscape still thick with snow.

Boulders of snowdrifts trim its edge,
where the undulating tracks of deer
follow an uncertain border
trusting the ice for miles
until, at last, on the far shore
I see its conclusion:
the floral blush of kill on the riverbank
and the tracks of coming and going –
the blunt traffic of death.

And, unexpectedly, there it is:
how everything is traffic
how we didn't always get along
when we were children
but time insists on surrender
and relief, its faithful ally.
It insists, especially, on love.
It leaves more room.

The train is taking me home at last.

My tears confuse me
because they want to be joy and sorrow
at the same time.

Absolution

This morning in a great puddle at Freeman's
I watched the crow bathe,
tossing water over his wings
like his own blessing
his own absolution.
I laughed, hidden in my home.
All this wakefulness, at last.

And tonight, at dinner
he returns with his entourage
and they are excavating the compost
then crossing the mowed lawn
like old bowlegged men.
They listen for the slow
thrust and shudder of worms
and move on.
I step out to toss the dishwater into the perennials
and the black bodies rise from the compost
and wheel away except for one:
he perches in the elm
and sharpens his beak on the rough bark
while I call out to him,
telling him how lovely he is.

Longing

I'm taking a break from longing
so the fog can wait
and ply its uncanny voltage on someone else
and the yellow forsythia can distill its colour
without me noticing.
I will walk by and not be astonished.

When I pass, I will nod politely to the magnolias
as though their buds were not dipped
in late afternoon light
and their woolen pods were not thick
with the pulp of new life
and the robin's breast
was not bulging and thrusting forth,
building invitation and warning into the same song.

I'm taking a break from longing.
This way I can walk home in peace
and the cannons firing off in my heart
will be stilled when I reach the dim hallway
that leads up to my tiny apartment,
that cloistered space
where the sound of the ticking clock
rattles the windows.

Spring Walk

for Mom

Last spring we walked to the village
and stopped to study the migration
of a mother skunk
with her trail of babies following,
their steps and movements
an orchestra of canopied tails.

The way they rolled and wove their way
around her body
rooted us to the spot
and they crossed the road,
and then began
weaving the tall grasses
through Jimmy's long hayfield
and we continued watching them
long after they had been swallowed
by the meadow,
their progress puncturing the stalks
with sway and gentle pivoting
almost imperceptible
unless you knew
what you were looking for.

Conversation with the Night Air

The sea, that old rattle,
is chasing the wind up the hill,
is pushing at the curtains again.
Its exhale
propels the fabric
and lifts it into the air.

Whose great breath this
that pulls the bedroom curtains
in and out like lungs breathing?
Whose dilated pulse?

Once we were perfect in the world
but time has run away with the sea.
It will always do that.

My hands are my father's now
but less papery; time
has not finished working them over.

My father's hands! So large and gentle,
scribing notes to me from far away.
I collect each word because it is his handwriting
even though history is ephemeral.

The wind's chorus tells me so,
its orchestral movements
snatching at the night air.

Evidence

In digging up the property
for gardens
more pottery is unearthed:
rusty nails, a partial set of teeth.
I am on someone else's life
creating new.
That is what it is, after all:
these layered lives
we come and go,
emptying our pockets into the earth
the keeper of our rust
our stories.

We have all been here before
when we were someone else.

Sermon: Everything Tries to be Round

Tonight I stand under the membrane of the sky.
So many stars!
They stretch along the hill behind the house,
a canopy that I can trace
from the root of the spruce trees
twitching beneath the boughs
to the mighty bowl overhead
telling stories of how round the earth really is.

Down below in the bay
water is wreathing the rocks –
they too have their own roundness,
and the place where roundness is meant to find itself.

Just watch the way the tide rolls up to a rock
and surrounds it, then tugs away again and again:
forever making proclamations to roundness.

Everything that goes away
comes back again.
Everything that comes
goes away.

This is my faith,
my big round ball of faith:
the roundness of cupped hands –
hands that are always full.

Pied Piper

When I was a child
my grandfather's whistling would call us
out of a quiet summer reverie
and we'd scramble through the neighbour's field
along the well-worn path up the hill
to arrive at the open barn door
with its one hollowed step.
Inside, he stood at his workbench
where the smell of oil was buried in wood
the brows of the barn boards
were creased with sunlight and dust motes
the big stillness collecting sound in the rafters.

His whistling song
greened grass and sweetened water;
the vibrato rising from his pursed lips ripened fruit:
the raspberries, filled with self-approbation,
would drop from heavy branches.
The strawberries, between manicured rows of straw,
were induced to succulence and ripened overnight.
In late summer, the pear tree
invited the long ladder from the barn
while impatient pears threw themselves
from great heights
to land in our mothers' waiting aprons
or straw baskets.
Even the wasps, languid with feeding,
politely detached and bowed to the industry
of our harvest.

But that was long ago.
Now my grandfather is below the ground,
a kilometre away from the farm.
Long have his bones rested there.
Every year, his grandchildren visit the cemetery,
our feet playing another tattoo
to the long story of bones,
the sound they make when they are nested in the earth.

Potato Crop

Where are the old trains?
I want one in particular –
the one that passed through Fulford
when my grandmother was a young woman.

It blundered through the town,
jerking and squealing in the night
braking over loose ties and splintered creosote
waking everyone, and then it derailed
spilling carloads of potatoes into the valley.
Everyone, blind to threats of the authorities,
who would have that bounty bleed into the earth,
gathered the fallen harvest
in baskets and aluminum pots.

This is the train my grandmother
thanks for feeding the whole village.
I want that one.
But not necessarily here.

I want the train tracks
to spring out of joists in villages everywhere,
everywhere there is a town with empty fists,
so that they must fill them,
drop whatever they may have been holding
for years
and lift potatoes into their palms:
the perfect essay to hunger.

Let there be the potatoes my grandmother
picked up in the woods
and in the valley where they rolled
hidden in the tall summer grasses.

Fenian Raid

During the Fenian Raids along the border
between Quebec and Vermont
Margaret would fetch water from the silent river
to home
her daily task for her father
a defining stillness in the land, always, for her
and a play of light along the edges of oak leaves
that couldn't speak
and the lost activity of bees in the fields
and how the river could be so busy with movement
and nothing else
just movement built on flashes of colour,
where water would fold in on itself
coiling around rock and blurring the edges of the bank.

My father has taken me to her grave on Eccles Road.
There's a monument for her there
her valiant life, those spilled buckets of water
when the soldiers called her to halt
and she didn't hear a thing.

I think about her sometimes,
about what sound might mean
when an ear is only a sheltering outcrop
that masks an inner cave;
how voice is where our experiences get archived
and how we tether our history to that cadence;
a drumbeat, a drone, a prescience
that would have been tuned to the shuffling of soldiers
their guns poised and ready,
waiting on the river's edge.

Rising Moon

How do the trees experience the moon –
the way it sheds them when it rises
the way they are burnished with light, then not?
Tonight I watch it inflate over the hill
behind the house – shredding the tattered clouds
until, unfurled, it owns the empty sky.
The crickets are still talking about it
even though it is dark and the dew has set.
My clothes are musk-spangled, sequined in light.
The trees in the yard, the aspen, the fir
and the dappled maple, stand in awe.
They know this holiness as a fond friend.
Even the waves hitting the shore below: applause.
We remember to be beloved of the earth.

Starfish

We were walking the deserted cove off Gegogan
where we'd anchored the boat
when I found the sea star in the shallows
and lifted it for closer consideration.
It settled into my hand.

I moved to show my sister
feeling the aliveness of it
and looked down again to find
that it was rippling with life
that was not its own.
Small sea lice
had animated it
and they moved about its leggy chambers
filling it with new opportunity.

I placed it back in the sea,
all day marvelling
at the pulse of life in death
the understanding that, always,
there will be tenants waiting
to inhabit the unoccupied shell we have abandoned
after we have been battered by a rough sea
or softened by time.

I am surprised all day long.

At Last: the Bees

Finally they come
tentative, a few scattered in the garden
almost haphazard in the humid air
and the summer coughing out its slow recline.

This morning the flowering thyme
moved slightly with visitors
those soft pads lighting on the vibrating bushes
bursting with the electricity
of hasty pollination everywhere
the spirea giddy with pink welcome cups
we are all waiting
breathless for the sweet assault
the heavy black legs
weighted with yellow powdered gifts.

Oh, come and feed us all.

The Constellations

for Jim

As children we rooted our grubby hands
to the forest floor and clawed at the earth
so the sweet pungent smell would stay with us;
we'd lay on the stone wall like it was a cold pyre
waiting for a match to spark the night
and then we'd climb poplars and bend with them
wildly careening through a wider space.

At night we riddled with the stars on the lawn
in grasses sweetened with our easy warmth
the summer sky punctured with distant torches.
I held onto your every word in the dark
while the numberless stars turned and tuned
as if reception was improved with the naming:
Orion. Ursa Minor. Ursa Major.

Kitchen Songs

All day tirelessly the mother robin
feeds her trailing fledgling
up and down the hill.
Off the porch
from the lower branches of the elm
to its base he follows obediently
unlearning his helplessness.

And all day I am in the kitchen
cooking lemon loaf and gingersnaps
harvesting the garlic scapes
and sinking them into cupcakes of olive oil
to the tune of this loveliness.

And the damp laundry:
two loads come in off the line
to be draped everywhere
the battlemented house
of fog-weary linens.

And the six or eight pans
of dirty dishes
the hiccup of the second hand
on the clock
all the while
such timelessness, this
such knowing and trembling and awe.

I have been happy a thousand times today.

Capitulation

It has happened: the peonies have succumbed.
Before daybreak, the early thunderstorms
rattled and lumbered up and down the hill
and forced those heavy heads, at last, to earth.
In the day's newest incarnation
their shattered bodies rest in the grass;
balls of pink giving way to gravity's
seductive pull, its unhurried consumption.

Meanwhile the skies brighten to new pursuits:
the rabbits make clover heads disappear,
head by white head, and the jays instigate
from the dampened hearts of lower branches.
The orange hawkweed, still shrunken and wet,
wipe heavy raindrops from their scruffy crowns.

What We Leave Behind

A thousand small tasks and the day is done.
Bequeathed to us:
the aftermath of measureless deeds.
Was I kind enough?
Attentive enough?
Did I note my walk to the mailbox
or the heft of the lock on the shed door?
Did I consider the salvaged fishing net
now landlocked
around my vegetable garden
or the skin on my arms turning to aging silk
the remembrance of friends gone
and what they leave behind:
paintings and recipes
and books initialled.

This morning I marvelled at the tiny husks
I found in the corner of the living room
what the spider left behind.

And later, such truths compounded
with the spider nest I spilled into the lawn
catapulting hundreds of little bodies
into a foreign terrain
causing them to be suddenly, unexpectedly
like us, over and over again
bereft of location and knowable landmarks.

Ancestry

Wine Harbour
has coughed ashore
enough mottled earth shells
for me to collect forever:
ochre and red
white like teeth
greens that are carved from spring grass
or young kelp.

I gather them wanting
always wanting
to throw myself down
onto the rocks
and muster my old, old self,
the one that crawled out of the sea
millions of years ago.

Translations

Sometimes the world has to reimagine itself
in another language we did not create:
today it comes as the charge of the hummingbirds
thrusting their beaks at each other
so I can hear them across the yard
the clashing of little sticks
and squeaking hinges.

Meanwhile, in the west
the sky thickens with angry thunderheads
the garden holds its breath
the clock on the wall
doesn't skip a beat
that patient, dogged tyrant of unwind.

Everything participates:
the way the land surrenders
to the principles of gravity
and acquiescence, the oldest language.

Permission. I am granted more days, more time,
more participation in the world

so I do: participate and surrender.

Did you see how the wild roses
cupped their pink petals open
like the palm of a hand,
like the shell on the beach
receiving the salt and sand?

How they cast their scent over the yard recklessly
beseeching the wasps to further vigour?

Did you see the black crow pause
in the grass and stare between his twig feet
waiting to hear the worm,
all he had to say
in his stealth to transformation?

All of this. It is always enough.

I surrender, surrender, surrender.

Every moment for some is a villain,
something they were owed
while we walked on ahead.
I don't know what to tell them anymore.

Do you hear the trembling aspen trees?
Listen to their words!
They are whispering the melody of the coming storm
just now on the lake
moving up the hill.

Porcupine

for Shelley

Last week we walked along the road
and came upon a dead porcupine in the bend

It was in the looking back
that we both clung to each other:
his perfect feet were
upturned against the asphalt in supplication,
the little pads facing us
like the crooked feet of a child
kneeling for nightly prayer
before crawling under safe covers

What do we know about love?
It carries in it the decay of understanding
even as it flowers out of our breasts

And what of the porcupine's
attentive plodding
across a field of clover in mid-summer
or the breath that filled his small frame every day?
Who, then, is the keeper of his stories:
the nights when he climbed the neighbour's apple tree
and gorged himself on fruit until the branches
sagged beneath his weight?

Where do those stories go?

Don't they count?

Last night I retraced my steps
and bent over what was left of his little body,
marvelling at the remnant of spine and the fine bones;
the quills that fanned into the gravel on the roadside

all this hastening to death everywhere
like so much forgotten narrative
that longs to talk about love
but hasn't the words.

Composition

1.

How light falls on things
is what we learn when the morning rain
has redeemed seaweed
or bent water into thistles:
shapes joining shapes
so that what becomes important
is where the edges mix;
dark and light
is where the skeleton of composition hides
and where pigments find each other.

2.

The ocean grabs at the coast
where a tripod of women
is weaving its edge with their stooping,
the flow of light coming in and out.
They are mottled information,
sun on barnacled skin
the movement that keeps light in:
lucky accidents of history
the landscape of woman
along such a lonesome shore.

3.

It is the light, just now, that surprises me
inviting itself to the surfaces of leaves
brocading the trees with thick strokes
so that, when I move indoors, I steal first:
plucking leaves where the light has collected
imagining myself eating them
that I might glow from within
the way Sarah did
when the firefly got trapped in her ear
the way it throbbed its little light there
the core of her being quietly aglow
the firefly safe and stowed in warm silence,
the way so much light
gets stored inside.

4.

There are nameable things
like the delphiniums that blush a deeper blue
in summer night air
flowers that squander themselves
on the grey canvases
of uncompromising skies.
It doesn't matter:
like watercolours, they search
for the light place
that goes into light.
So many fugitive colours!

5.

Let's start with what we cannot name.
I think about love and
how to speak it on paper,
and if I could melt
into the swelling bushes along the berm
I would be three-dimensional
in atmospheric space.
I'd call that a good lesson in paint
where tension at the edges
would be
only about flowers.

Maple Tree in July

for Susan

The air is as heavy as tired arms
and even the maple tree sags under the weight of it.
We pause outside, noting
the hulk of a thunderhead on the horizon,
half beckoning with its promise of rain
and our unspoken wish
cajoling it to further enterprise.

On the path to the building,
I am distracted by a clutch of maple helicopters
fastened together like a bouquet for a child's small hand
and I pick it up and hold it.

We study the way its sun-bleached skin has softened
to the brown of a doe's coat
and underneath, if it could have an underbelly,
it is safe with the ripeness of spring green
still captive and protected
despite the withering heat of July.

It is my wish to believe the folly of negligence
greater than the folly of metaphor:
look at our hands veined with time's sweet shadows!
how they ripen
the same way those tireless helicopters
dedicate themselves to season
and the way we store narrative
in the tall silos of our breasts
the same way bark on a maple tree
grapples with its own vigorous history.

Kitchen Spider

All summer
in the kitchen
this spider
this small black bead has watched me
from the corner
where the shelf meets the wall
and all summer, at my hand: clemency.
Oh, to wield such power
over his dedicated industry!

Tonight I blew gently on his web
and he cowered –
this too, a power and a cruelty
when really, I want to praise him,
praise his diligence and daring,
praise the slow sprawl of his web
the desiccated husks of insects
those brittle accordioned relics of ant and fly
the mystery of their revision
beneath him, twisted
in the old lattice of strings.

What sense the too-neat house
when I have the company
of this worker by my side?
Clemency indeed.
He grants me his own generous portion
of the same.
I am better for his presence.

Late Messengers

Time wants to hold your hand
and until you open your palm
and surrender to the truth:
that we all die,
Until then, everything else
is a story someone is reading to you.

There is nothing else to say.

The moon will rise tonight,
the stars will blink their stories
even as their message comes
after their own death,
travelling forward to us
over vast spaces of time.
Are we like that? Late messengers?
Who, in the very depths of our outlaw selves,
did we break away from
to travel all this way?

Tonight, I will step outside as usual
and listen to all that does not speak
and tune my ear to that loudness:
the stars with their unknowable erasure,
cancelling themselves into the future,
are inviting us to step into the sea of forever,
to drop into those disappearing constellations
that birthed us.

Come stand with me, unencumbered.
The love out there, it's so big.

Garlic Harvest

After the summer's cruel drought
they come reluctantly from the parched earth
tress-tousled, surrendering white filigree roots
feathered with dirt, to rest in the sun and dry.

This morning, tying them in sloppy bundles,
I marvel at the strength of each bulb,
the bone-white hardness filled out,
their sturdiness a knotted fist in my own.

Inside this nested congestion
a separate bud waits patiently,
its pungent endowment
a salute to the ripening of all things
on their way to transformation.
It is a progression we overlook in ourselves.

Oh, the bright goodness of those white knuckles!
It is enough to weaken my knees with gratitude.

September Morning

This morning the fog is lifting
and the spiders have shot wires
of stringed light
across the yard
vast stretches of tightrope
that the sun is now introducing
to this new, uncut day.

I step out barefoot
and the sharp cold grass of September
fires my feet
and sends me into the garden
where one web is white clotted cream
tagging a line between
the brown stems of tired perennials
the bright light its own portal
to new thought
helping me to reimagine my day.

Perspective

Nights like these when I am walking home
and the faintest breeze
lifts its autumn anthem into my senses,
I want time inverted briefly,
the way the spider crossing the ceiling of my bedroom
can have two worlds at once:
what is here and what is there.

I would choose there:
to look down on the smudge of maple trees
in a familiar landscape,
the field behind my parents' home
where we held imagined prisoners
on the great humpbacked boulders
the tips of the birches
we abused with our careless weight
now, from above, reduced to spired pinpricks.

Then the road ribboning down to my aunt's store
with its hollowed stoop sun-warmed to our grubby feet
and finally the Yamaska River parched,
shrunken to a creek on those dry summer days
when we would wade across the shallows
on feet that could have been webbed,
turning over rocks to see what might live there.

September Rain

The rain has beaded on Vi's long hair.
It softens us both while the tide surges
beyond Sonora into a wider Atlantic trail.
The white breakers swell into currents
and the warblers in the apple tree
skip from wet goldenrod
to heavy branches and back again
singing the song we all are feeling
with the belated rain at last,
their cheeriness carrying up the hill
to us, mist-soaked and aging into the earth.

The fog has spackled the dusk with dull silver
so the strong pencil lines of the poplars
carve out last emblems of the day
before folding into shadow.

The earth is asking of me a devotion
and some days I forget to shed
the leaden heaviness of care –
despite those warblers and finches
flouncing over the sloping hills
who are not asking anything of the world
but an ongoingness of mist, perhaps,
or a singular dedication to the apple tree just there.

Finally, as I step to the car,
the clumps of black flies
spiral out of their own tornado
and sweep past us
funnelling into the grey sky.

Behind us, Jo nickers from the barn stall.

How can I ever think I am not happy?

Black Brook on Friday

We step into moss-mottled woods, roots uprooted
their stiff frayed fingers against packed earth
our voices slightly louder in answer
to the falls, the forest sugared with the
first treasonous snow of winter. We find
our way to the rope line tagging the trees
down to the river, to the quiet pools
below the falls. We trace the slate shoreline
until we are in the underbelly
of high voltage movement and tarnished light
our conversation jousting with volume
and empty ovations, hands and noses cold
the wall of water tumbling beside us
making us first smaller, then nothing, and complete.

The End of Birds

It was only last week my aunt
stood by the bird feeder
holding sunflower seeds in an open palm
and the chickadees stepped onto her hand,
their feet like breakable twigs.

But then there was Mom's cat
crouched in the driveway
with a mourning dove in her mouth
until she yowled to show off her prize
and the bird just sat there
dull and stupid – its willful blindness;
the darkening stare: we became the fading sepia print
as we bent to inspect the wound
and the driveway thrummed with feathers
emptying from its back.

It was also the way Bill lifted his arms,
wrenched them in mid-air with an added twist
to show how he snapped the partridge's neck.

Even in Vermont last summer, birds were hit by cars,
each tidy projectile propelled neatly
into the new hay in the ditches
where their heads flopped over like drowsy passengers
on a bus heading home.

Finally there was the old man
outside the café on Sherbrooke Street,
his face grafted with shiny new patchwork skin,
who dropped pastry crumbs on the pavement
and his laughter scratched the afternoon
while the birds fell out of nowhere.

Dusk on Cameron Road

The water puddles along the shore
its own quietness ballooning around us.
We take the old trail back, the one
that is a black yawning hole in the distance.
But when we enter the darkened path
the moss is thick and green,
a dozen colours my hand needs to touch.

Then the sharp stab of white –
a long diagonal across the trail
a fallen birch we consider and climb over.
And around the base of trees, great pools of water,
one that calls me back for a second look
because it has taken the sky
and dropped it into the earth just there
and I pause to find it reflecting up.
We talk quietly. Not a lot, not wanting
to interrupt the trail, its knowing,
the plants tending to their own vigorous stories.

Turning the Clocks Back

It catches us sideways, that fresh hour we lost.
Now broken shards of light cut the bare fields.
This time of year the remaining birds, backlit,
slanted by autumn's light, then reinvented
become obscure in this ruddy season.
The trees throw splinters of light at us,
the ocean is no longer blue and inviting
but hard cobalt, the colour of an ice-glazed pond.
The sumac goes off to war in red
clashing against a sharpening sky.
The ripened apples, pregnant and bursting,
drop to the ground, become hulking red stones
on a mottled lawn where the crows descend
and pierce their pulpy hearts with eager beaks.

Carol and France

There they go, off into the night,
my sister and her beloved with their dog.
Their flashlight smudges against the sky then drops
while they walk and, as I imagine, talk.

The moon is a cleft stone, almost in darkness
but its underside is on fire to match
the horizon, still skimmed in floral pinks.
Our commentary travels between us
as they disappear down the road.
Then the cold night air sends me in to close blinds
and wait upstairs until their light comes on.

How good and familiar their love is
and what a relief that tonight
I feel illuminated by it
and not bereft or alone.
There is enough love in me to love theirs.

October in Fulford

Before the next symphony of water falls on us
I work outside, the soil rich in my hands
the quiet earth pretending dormancy.
Beside me, the mighty trunks of the poplars
emboldened by age, and impervious
to the old story of our climbing
and our flexing of their young bodies
now are freighted with time and girth
while I am shrunken, earth-planted and awed
at all they do not tell, all there is to forgive.
And deeper in the woods, through those tall columns
I see two trees upended, the earth blossom
now a black blot in the forest, tilted trunks
addressing the ground in unexpected angles.

In the Basement

Today, cleaning up my parents' basement
I find an old board
that we laid claim to as children
our names, our wishes
etched into it.
How childish and earnest and lovely we were.

And the basement, each day I work there
is ripening with memory
the pillars of cement we played on
and up in the floor joists
the word "peace" etched in bold
even then such hopeful wishes
for the world
I keep finding myself, almost,
but not quite,
that little girl who loved this unruly world
even then.

Crow

for Cher

In the neighbour's field the afternoon sun
has turned the grass to gold.
The crow stands in a sea of bent stalks
and basks in the light of late day;
his coat of feathers flashes black and slick.
He pauses often in the breadth of this one day
this great Now
the weight of his participation
knowable to the field
to the sky
and to the grasses.

Who can say this is not true?
We make our own truths every day
and declaim for all creatures and plants
who do not speak our tongue.
They are voiceless
those who do not use language the way we do.

Reckless words!
Give me the jaunty swagger of a crow
in late November's field
when the sun's last song
makes the shadows race up the back hill.
He knows better than we do:
everything that matters is in his crooked feet
just now settling in the cool grass.

At Elizabeth Bishop House

I: Imminence

Outside Elizabeth Bishop House
starlings, those weather heralds, are flocking,
hastening after the last vital goodness
in the tired grasses, before the heavy snow descends.
They bob in the field between haggard cedars
that spike skywards, where ample vacancies wait.
In the distance, the Bay of Fundy,
mud-scudded, both darkens and lightens
sporting with the grey imminence of storm.
The birds, sloppy schoolchildren, drop closer
to the house, to my window view and then,
as if tuned to my intrusive pencil scratch,
they take flight and land in a further field,
heads nodding to usher in the first winter storm.

II: Shattered Nest

No, I mean the one outside in the tree
that gazes back from the upstairs window.
Shattered by November's muscular winds
it flaps in a sun-riddled sky today
a post-storm membrane in the branch fingers.

Below, abandoned birdhouses gape,
open-mouthed, upside down against the trunk
a season's demolition, the early cull
of autumn's predictable thrust and tug.
Yesterday's fickle starlings are long gone
annexed to other seed-studded grasses.
The house rumbles now and warms itself
in the polished light. I sift through my pages,
long conversations with other broken women.

While Crossing the Field

for Sandy

Today in November's fading garden
a female cardinal surprises us,
that bright beak amongst the bossy jays:
a coral and flax stab of restrained light
in the midst of rowdy blue baubles.

Then the walk through the gold saturated field
where the wind has teased the drowsy grasses
into sloppy tufts, so many yellow dunes
ignited against a sharp sky,
beside me, your companionable presence
its own billowing season in my heart.
On our path: the remainder feathers
of the dead pheasant bookmark the trail,
reminder of gloss and its sidekick, fugitive time.

January Moon in Fulford

for Mom

The moon finds its old channels to fullness
breaking paths through the bulk of the city
monolith shards fracturing its steady light.
It rises out of the fertile escarpment
that once was the Champlain Sea, until
when my car stops at last in the country,
it has cleared the maples along the driveway.

At eleven, we turn off all the lights
and consider the snowy moonscape,
what it takes away and gives back transformed:
daylight at night, cobbled boulders behind the house
sleeping against winter's latest prank,
this earliest satellite oiling the fields.
We are awed by its eternal statement.

The Otter

Bev and I stand in her kitchen
where the January light
is firing through the orange jelly jars
on the windowsill
the sun's brightness
making us crouch and squint
to find the otter on the ice.

Then there he is: sleek and glistening
against an impossible cold.
The blue ice on the bay
has buckled.
Now it is hummocky
where the wind has forced it
to renew itself.

The otter is rippling along the ice
brown and slick
beyond the fir trees
that unfurl shadow and light
in the wind.

At last we move away
from the window
and I think,
Oh yes, this is happiness –
mine and the otter's
the generosity of the light today
how much room it holds!

The stillness in the heart just now,
the everything of this one moment,
wanting the great Now
and nothing else.

Lost Language

My words are looking for a place to be
and they won't settle.
There is the shed roof, tiles lifting
and moss-mottled,
the windfalls from this winter's storm,
the wrinkled landscape of low tide.
Or the way the birds wake me
this time of year
or the unexpected flowers
on an old plant in the front porch.
Everything wanting to burn brightly
and say to me:
This is where your thoughts want to rest
where the roses, soon to fill out,
remember everything they need to say.

Acknowledgements

I am deeply grateful to Harry Thurston for long believing in my voice, for pausing with me in the road over a year ago and saying, "Deborah, it is time." Heartfelt thanks for being my first reader. I am indebted to Viola Burns for her keen and enthusiastic consideration of my manuscript.

To the team at Pottersfield Press, thank you all: Lesley Choyce for your guidance, Julia Swan for your diligence with my writing and the warmth of your collaboration, Gail LeBlanc and Peggy Amirault for the elegant cover and layout design.

Much gratitude to the Elizabeth Bishop Society of Nova Scotia and its community of women who ensured that I had the opportunity to work in the profound stillness of EB House.

To family and friends in Nova Scotia and Quebec, thank you all. And special thanks to Sandy for banner-waving, long walks, and even longer conversations.

About the Author

Deborah Banks was born into a large family and raised in Fulford, in the Eastern Townships of Quebec. She studied English and Education at Bishops University. Her teaching career spanned thirty-four years and included experiences in rural Quebec, Northern Quebec, and Montreal.

Her parents first introduced her to Nova Scotia as a child, and the die was cast. Twenty years ago she purchased an abandoned house there with the intention of making it her permanent residence.

In 2018, Deborah initiated Poem in Your Pocket Day in her community in Sherbrooke, Nova Scotia, a national event which encourages people to share and recite poetry at work, in schools, and on the street. She has led poetry workshops in Quebec and Nova Scotia.

Deborah has been writing poems ever since she was a child. Her poetry and essays have appeared in *The New Quarterly, Matrix, The Globe and Mail,* and *The Montreal Gazette,* as well as several anthologies. Deborah's rural upbringing informed her sensibilities and her engagement with the natural world. The work of Mary Oliver enhanced her devotion to all things wild and beautiful.

Deborah Banks lives in Port Hilford, Nova Scotia.